GW00391109

Published by McNaughty Books, an imprint of John Napir Ltd
P.O.Box 3353. London N1 1SR

© MVM Cathy Hopkins

Cartoons © Alison Everitt

ISBN 1-898505-05-5

Printed and bound in the U.K.

HOW TO BE
A POLITICALLY CORRECT
SEX MANIAC

by JOHNNY CONDOM

CONTENTS

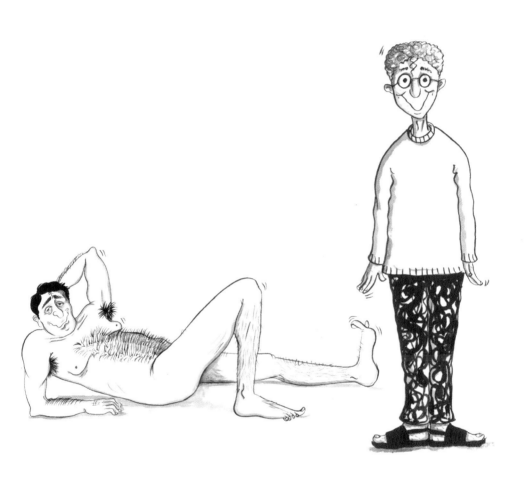

Question: Which of these chappies needs this book the most?
Answer: Both need all the help they can get.

Introduction

The trouble all started back in the Garden of Eden.
'I'm in charge cos I came first' proclaimed Adam.
'And have done ever since' sighed Eve wearily.

Well, a lot of water's flowed under the bridge since then and many battles fought and won but just lately the chaps have taken a bit of extra hammering. They've been criticised for bad behaviour from the bedroom to the board room and admonished for putting their noses (and other parts of their anatomy) where they didn't belong.

Inevitably, this has left a good few lads feeling confused, like they can never get it right. What do women want? More than a few decided that the best course of action was to keep their mouths shut, retreat from the fray a while and watch from a safe distance while certain changes took place.

Changes like:
1. Girls deciding that anyone with a todger was the enemy.
2. Girls changing their minds and deciding that some chaps were OK after all.
3. Girls deciding they don't like the new age variety, men should be men (as long as they wash up sometimes.)
4. Girls fighting for equality. And rightly so. (Though they still expect a chap to pick up the lunch cheque.)

The lads didn't decide anything through all this. As always, they mainly want to get laid and girls still call the shots.

This book is meant for any would be sex maniac out there who could do with a little help in rising to the challenge.

Tip No 1 for Boys

Watch which jokes you laugh at.
This can score you points or not.

Not OK jokes. (So keep a straight face.)
1. **Question:** How do you make a feminist smile?
   Answer: Shove a coat hanger in her mouth

2. **First salesman:** why do 98 percent of men have an orgasm every time they have sex whereas only two percent of women do?
   Second salesman: Who cares?

OK Jokes. (Fall about laughing.)
1. **Question:** Why are men like footballers?
   Answer: Cos they both dribble when they're trying to score

2. **Question:** What's the similarity between most men and a cheap firework display?
   Answer: One mediocre bang and the evening's over.

Get it?
Girls can laugh at men and be derogatory about them but men can't laugh at girls (at least not within earshot and not if they want to get their legover.)

GETTING READY

Apparently first impressions are made in the first thirty seconds that someone sees you. So wait a minute before you make an entrance.

The bad news:

According to a recent survey, women like men with:
a small butt, slim body, flat stomach, sexy eyes, long legs, tall frame, muscular chest and shoulders and all his own hair.

The good news.

Top on their list is a sense of humour.
Make her laugh, tell her you have got all the above but that they're all in your other car. Which is a Porsche.

Man with his own hair

Clothes:

Your clothes say everything about you, so best put on a disguise. As clothes are absolutely a matter of personal taste, it's hard to pin down any hard and fast rules except that it's always advisable to:
* keep outfits simple
* keep them clean.
* wear trousers that fit properly

Don't wear:
* Smelly socks
* T shirts with funny lines
* Baggy Y fronts
* Open shirts and gold medallions

Don't's:
Don't smother yourself in overpowering pong that smells like paint stripper with a dash of lemon
Don't wear the shirt you wore yesterday
Don't wear brown shoes with a grey suit
Don't give false expectations ie: forget about stick on hair chests, padding the privates
Don't wax your genitals

Check List

When you're dressed and ready, do a quick run through of what you may need when you're out.

* car keys
* clean underwear
* credit cards
* taxi firm's card (in case you get lucky or legless)
* bus pass (in case you don't)
* your English/Swedish dictionary (you may meet some Swedish girls and even if you don't, there's still the local girls. In your best sing song voice, try awful chat up lines like: 'Have you got some Svedish in you? No? vell, vould you like some?' You'll get away with it as she'll have no idea what you've said and probably be intrigued.
* wallet,
* toothbrush
* condoms
* good looks
* a sense of humour
* talent
* a miracle

What is sexy in a man

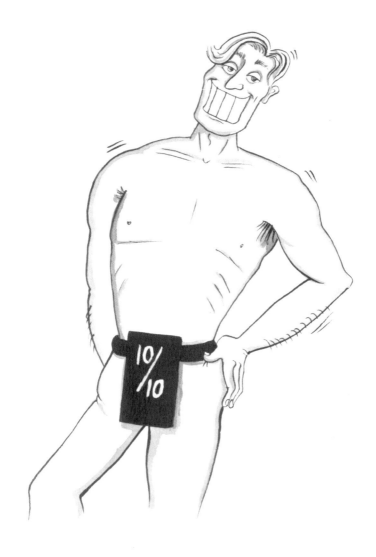

WHERE TO FIND GIRLS

Girls are everywhere. First you have to decide what sort of girls you want meet, then think about the sort of things she'd probably get up to in her time off, then look there. In the meantime, here's a few suggestions:

Great places to meet girls:
First nights/private viewings/gallery openings
Therapy nights/Self help seminars/Workshops
Video cassette stores
Work
Aerobics classes
Through friends
In a garden centre
Asda supermarket singles nights
Lassooing classes
Through dating agencies
Coming out of divorce courts
Alcoholics Anonymous.

Not such a great places to meet girls:

kd lang concerts
King's Cross
Telephone kiosks
Prenatal classes
Over the hill

HOW TO GET NOTICED
The Johnny Condom problem page

Question: How do I get noticed in the first place?
Johnny: Here's a few ideas:

DO:
1. Learn how to small talk. Chat about casual things, situations you both have in common. Keep it light and simple.
Right:
* How do you know so and so?
Wrong:
* How long have you had that cellulite?
* Can you lend me a tenner 'til my dole cheque comes in?
* How much do you charge?/And what do I get for that fiver?
2. Show her you can also be deep and interesting. That you are capable of philosophical thoughts like these:
* Where do all the lost socks go?
* What should you give a sick florist?
* How does the man who drives the snow plough get to work?
* If ghosts can walk through walls. How come they don't fall through the floor?
* What does Santa get for his mother?
3. At parties, offer to take the food or drinks round. You'll have a ready made opener.
4. Be yourself
5. Fall over her

6. Get a friend to point you out as someone to stay away from. She'll be intrigued as to why. He should say you always used to leave a trail of broken hearts wherever you went but now you've repented and are staying away from women for fear of being bad again. Your friend must say he's not convinced by your change of heart.

By now, she will want to know who you are, women are fascinated by reformed rogues and bad boys. You must be prepared to do the same for your friend but not with the same girl.

DON'T:

1. Don't talk non stop about yourself. Give her a chance.

Right:

Enough about me. What about you?

Wrong:

Enough about me. What about you? What do you think of me?

2. Don't take all your clothes off and do your gorilla impersonation

3. Don't follow her into the loo

4. Don't whistle at her

5. Don't moon at her

6. Don't rub up against her

7. Don't refer to her or any of her 'sisters' as: bikes, cock alleys, crack bats, fishbowls, fly traps, holes of content, love channels, manholes, meatgrinders, mole catchers, mousehole, mystic grottos, muffins, groundsheets, needle cases, organ grinders, pipe cleaners, saddles, toyshops, tuna, wick burner or pussy pieces.

They don't like it. Call them by their name although these days quite a few of them aren't averse to being called sir.

CHAT UP LINES

Question: What are the best chat up lines for girls?
Johnny: Forget about chat up lines. Premeditated clever lines tend to fall flat. Best relax, be yourself and try an opener like your wallet.

Don't try any of the following:
* Wanna come into the bushes and play with my mobile phone?
* Trust me I'm a doctor
* Drop 'em blossom you're on next.
* What do you use for painful piles?

The following is also a lousy chat up line but always worth it for the reaction.
YOU: I'm psychic. I bet I know what you're going to say next.
SHE: What?
YOU: That's amazing!

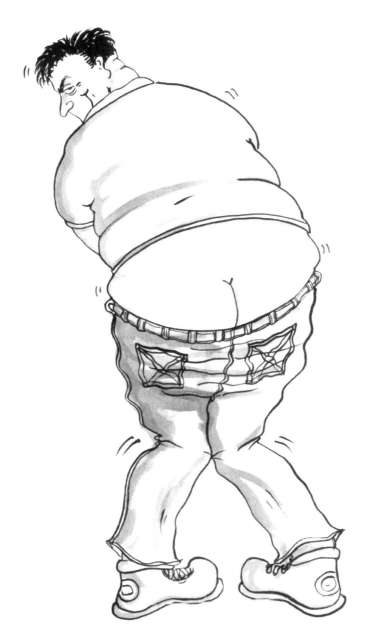

Not a recommended way to get noticed

ABOUT GIRLS:
(some questions answered)

Question: How do I know if she's the girl for me?
Johnny: Easy. All males are born with a built in compass. Which way is it pointing?

How to know if a girl is interested or not
Question: What do girls do if they don't like you?
Johnny: Ignore you and go home.
Question: What girls do if they do like you?
Johnny: Ignore you, go home and wait by the phone for you to call.
Confusing eh? This is only the beginning.

Question: Is it true that girls say yes when they mean no?
Johnny: Yes and no. I did a survey and asked twenty girls. "Yes" said the first ten. "No" said the others.

Question: How do I know if it's love, lust or anything in between?
Johnny: Simple.
Lust: is an excruciating horniness, like having an awful itch all the time.
Obsession: is when you have to call her. At 2am. Just to hear her voice.
A crush: you'd like to call her. But you're too scared.
Like: you'd like to date her. But you don't want to commit to anything
Love: you'll agree to anything

TECHNIQUES AND TYPES OF GIRLS

Many people think that there are only two types of girl:
1. The ones you want.
2. You ones you get.

Actually they all come in different shapes and sizes with different personalities. Quite often you get lots of different personalities in one girl depending on the time of month, the phase of the moon or her latest reading material.
Let me explain.

It is often said that when a man is alone in a room with a woman, actually there are three people present: - the man, the woman, and the man's willie which has a life and mind of its own.

Although this is so, it is also true that if man is alone in a room with a woman there can be as many as fifty people present as women are multifaceted, many layered, with lots of different personas which can do hourly shifts some days.
In plain English, schizoid.

The many sides of women

Here's just some of what can be her sub personalities: goodtime girl, princess, mystic, nympho, one of the lads, harlot, free spirit, poser, playmate, witch, intellectual, born again virgin, flirt, earth mother, slave, bossy knickers, feminist, bimbo, madonna, innocent, searcher, healer, saint, do gooder, babe, humanitarian.

No wonder women are such a mystery, which brings us onto the next big question.

Question: What do woman want?
Answer: In this order:
1. To eat as much chocolate as possible without getting fat
2. To be considered better looking than Michelle Pfieffer even if she looks like David Mellor
3. Equality in everything. Equal jobs, equal pay, equal orgasms.
4. A man with a heart of gold. And a knob like a milk bottle.

Question: What do men THINK women want?
Answer:
1. A good smack round the ear
2. To be men.

The second answer couldn't be more wrong. When this daft idea first came up, some poor unenlightened male dared to suggest that a lot of girl's aggression stems from penis envy. This is stupid. Most girls know that with what they've got they can get as many penis's as they like.

THE
ART OF FLIRTING

In the days of our ancient ancestors, flirting used to go like this.

He'd spot her marinating a bit of dinosaur breast, bang her over the head with his club and drag her off saying something romantic like "Brace yourself, I'm comin' in.'.

Later on in history, girls still used to get carried off but at this time, it was by knights on horseback.

In days of old
When knights were bold
The girls were really flirtie,
They'd blush and pout and put it out,
Not one of 'em got shirty
The girls were girls, the men were men,
But this is now and that was then.

Since then the rules seem to have changed, the roles got mixed. Girls won't let you carry them off any more and they've got better things to do than sitting around sewing, singing "hey nonny no" and polishing a chap's helmet.

A Viking's flirting technique

FLIRTING TIPS

DO:
* Be confident
* Make fleeting body contact
* Smile
* Be generous (a flirt'd never say 'do you want a drink? Yes me too, mine's a half')
* Be charming
* Make steady eye contact, then lower your gaze
* Keep it light.
    > **Right:** How are you? You look great.
    > **Wrong:** How are you? I'm a bit low tonight myself. I think I'm drinking too much. S'cos my folks split up when I was young which is probably why I always expect to get dumped. I've always felt a bit of a loser. Hey, let me tell you the whole story. It all started when I was four...
* Flatter the specific. All girls know what their attributes are therefore look carefully to see what they are, nice hair, great eyes, great legs? If you go in with some general line like ooh you're just gorgeous, she'll think you're bullshitting and that that is your standard line. However, if you notice what is unique about her, compliment that, she'll think you're on the line, have really noticed her and will give you brownie points.
* Make her feel special.
* Pay attention to her. There's nothing worse than someone talking to you and looking over your shoulder to see if any thing better's come in.

* Leave her wanting more so don't overstay your welcome
* Soften your voice. In general girls don't like loud men
* Be yourself. If you pretend to be something you're not, it can come back on you. For example, if she's a Rebecca and you say you're Jewish thinking it'll score you points, it might just work. You score. But later that night......

DON'T:
* Wait for someone else to make the move
* Look desperate
* Stand too close
* Brag. Girls don't like it. Get a friend to brag about you to her, that way it's acceptable.

He thinks: make eye contact: She thinks: run away.

Reading girls facial expressions and body language

1. Dilated pupils are sometimes a clue, it can mean,
a) Attraction. She's interested.
b) she's out of her head on ecstasy and everyone looks good

2. Extended eye contact can mean:
a) she likes the look of you.
b) she's short sighted and trying to work out if you're Keith from the filing department

3. Leaning towards you or in on you can mean:
a) she wants to be near you
b) she's blind drunk and can't stand up

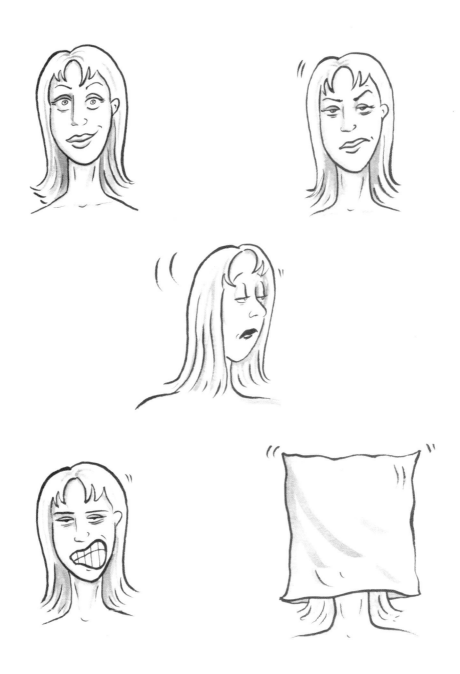

FIRST DATE

The art of dating is like dancing. Slow, slow, quick, quick slow. It's knowing when to be cool and when to be passionate. If you get the two mixed or mistimed you can blow the whole affair.

Be cool to start with. Don't pressurize.

Right:
He: Let's get together some time.
She: Sure. Next week?
He: Sounds good.

Wrong:
He: Let's get together?
She: Sure next week?
He: Why not now? Tonight. This is your big chance babe. Don't you like me? Take your clothes off. Please. Aw come on. I'm desperate.

Don't be desperate

Although it's said that when you're in love anywhere can be romantic, you can't use this as an excuse to be a cheapskate. First you have to get her to fall in love with you, so let atmospheres and ambiance work for you.

One book suggested getting a limo to pick her up for your first date then get the limo to pick you up outside somewhere impressive on route. A limo is out of reach of most people's budget but a taxi ride would be a nice gesture first time and probably score you a few points for consideration, and girls are big on that.

If you can't afford a taxi get your cousin Kev to do you a favour but get him to clean the car out first.

Don't get the taxi or Kev to pick you up outside:

* The dole office

* Bet's massage and sauna

* The local colonic irrigation centre

* The VD out patients clinic

* The local jail

It might give the wrong impression

Clean out the car
before your date

On your date:

DO:
Make some effort. How you behave with her in public will determine how she behaves with you in private

DON'T:
* Go if she asks if she can bring her
a) boyfriend
b) mother
c) rottweiller

* Book dinner too late in case she's a early night girl and is asleep at ten thirty.

* Go somewhere too famous or she'll be ogling movie stars and not you

* Shove your hand down her dress unless she invites you and even then I'd get her to put it in writing that she made the first move. A chap can never be too careful these days.

Small talk on first dates should be light, for example about theatre, travel, film or friends.

Lines to leave out of early conversations are:

* You remind me of mother. She's been dead ten years now.

* I'm hoping you'll help me decide once and for all if I'm bisexual, straight or gay

* Can you lend us a fiver cos I can't pay for our dinner

* I've decided not to go for good looking girls anymore, I'm going to settle for someone ordinary but loyal... like you

* I can't stop thinking about Gianni

* My analyst is dying to meet you

* My wife is in hospital having our third baby

* Ever thought of getting your teeth fixed?

NEW SPEAK

You may be able to speak in eight foreign languages but still not be able to master the female tongue. Too bad. She who must be obeyed is now she who must be understood. So catch up on the new speak.

NEW SPEAK TRANSLATIONS:
* In touch with your female side, means you can cry at sentimental bits at the cinema without being thought a big girl's blouse (It does not mean dressing up in girls lingerie)

* In touch with your inner child, means being aware of your emotional needs. (It does not mean: you still like to play games like doctors and nurses or cowboys and indians, in fact any games where she gets tied up)

* In lovemaking, vary your touch, means experimenting with positions and techniques. (It does not mean: try loads of different women)

* In lovemaking, taking your time, means fondling and foreplay. (It doesn't mean: have a sleep, a quick bang, then another sleep)

Man trying to get in touch
with his female side

Man trying to get in touch
with his inner child

* Fair play, means you are faithful and treat her like an equal. (It does not mean: once with a condom, once without)

* I'm not a materialistic person, means you're paying

* We're both adults, means if you don't agree with me you're childish

* I have found my male side, means I can be a controlling bugger and I've got a mean left hook

* I'm on a learning curve in my life, means I've haven't a flying f**k what I'm doing with my life

* I need space, means the kiss off, get lost. I want space any where where you're not.

* Sign language, means you sign for everything.

* Can we stay friends?, means no more sex, ever

* It wasn't you, means it **was** you

* You're a nice guy, I feel can really talk to you, means I can use you as an unpaid shrink while I offload about all the bad boy shits I'm dating

Some useful definitions according to girls
Romantic
Is: Spending loads of money on her
Isn't: Giving her a lift home after you've had sex
Getting out of the bath to pee

Consideration
Is: Taking into account her feelings
Isn't: Asking her husband if it's OK to sleep with her

Commitment
Is: not going with other girls when you're going out with her
Isn't: OK I'll stay the night.

When she says: "I have the heart of a young girl," she means that she is young and carefree and will probably want you to be the same. It does not mean: she is a psycho who has the heart of a young girl in a jar at home on her mantelpiece

When she says "I think we should be free to date other people," it means, she already is.

And finally Johnny Cash is a singer, not change from the condom machine. Oh yeah and don't yawn, say yes dear or laugh when she's being sincere.

ASTROLOGY
and REINCARNATION

Learn to listen. Girls are often into loads of weird stuff like therapy, finding their inner child, astrology and clairvoyants. Learn to deal with it. It could be the make or break.

Let me explain:
Wrong:
SHE: What sign are you Johnny?
HE: Oh Jesus. I dunno. You're not into astrology are you? S'all crap. A rip off
Exit girl

Right:
SHE: What sign are you Johnny?
HE: Aquarian. What are you?
SHE: Libra.
HE: Oh great. I read somewhere that they're good together. Let's read our horoscopes and see what the stars say about our future.

As this is so important, here's another example to make sure you really got it:

Amateur sex maniac:
SHE: I believe in a previous life I was a red indian squaw.
HE: You ought to be locked up. Weirdo.
Exit girl.

Pro sex maniac:
SHE: I believe I was a Red Indian squaw in a previous life.
HE: Wow. Really! What a coincidence. I was a big chief. Big Chief Spanking Whazza. Hey let's look into my crystal ball and see if we have a life together this time round.

HOW TO BE
A GREAT KISSER

When it comes to kissing, the idea is to get so good at it, you can do it with your eyes closed. This of course, like all aspects of the being a sex maniac, takes practise.
In the meantime, here's a few handy tips.

DON'T:
* Don't suck. You're not cleaning the drains.
* Don't hoover, slosh, mash, slaver, dribble, peck or gob.
* Don't open your mouth too wide. Wet car wash kisses are number one on the unpopularity scale.
* Don't keep your mouth too tight shut either. At that romantic moment, no-one wants to see a face coming at them with a mouth puckered up to resemble a cat's bottom.

* Don't get her in a position where she can't breathe
* Don't ram your tongue down her throat, even if you lose your chewing gum. Sometimes in life you have to be philosophical and just let things go
* Don't bite her head no matter how carried away you get.
* Don't eat onions, garlic, curries or tuna before hand unless you want to ditch her in which case it's quite a clever ploy and one guaranteed to work.

DO:
* Have clean breath
* Vary the intensity of your kisses from gentle to more searching, back again to gentle, to more passionate, to hello sailor, tonight's the night.

Warning:
1. Hot kisses can melt gold fillings

2. If a girl asks if she's the first girl you've ever kissed,
Say:
"Yes."
Don't add "and by far the best looking."
Never say:
"You might be. You do look familiar."

3. If she swears she's a virgin who's never been kissed before, get rid of her. Nice girls don't swear.

How to interpret kisses:
Cold nose - it's only puppy love
Sticky kisses - she's a stamp collector
Burning kisses - one of you's still got a cigarette in your mouth
Red hot kisses - one of you uses paprika lipstick (let's assume it's the girl)

And remember, the first kiss with someone is always the hardest. Like getting the first olive out of a jar, once you got that first one the rest come easily.

SEDUCTION APHRODISIACS

Moving on from kissing as one does, the next step is seduction. The first thing to remember when it comes to girls is that you have to get them to feel that you respect them. This is done by the stimulation of their main erogenous zone which is a large organ quite wide in dimension and commonly known as a brain.

With this is mind here are a few guaranteed turn ons for them:

Turn ons:
* 24 hours unlimited use of your credit card
* Your own chat show
* A Mercedes Benz
* Flattery (another word for this is foreplay, some girls are more than happy if you just admire them for twenty minutes or so, so forget about massaging toes and elbow, gently nibbling the neck. Go for the ears)

Don't say
* My ex had a body like Elle Mc Pherson
* Do you believe herpes really is contagious?

Don't say any of the following if she's acting a bit odd (all girls do from time to time)
* Is it your period?
* Oh. Here we go.
* Do you keep a list?
* Pardon me if I breathe.

Turn offs:
* Ex girlfriends lingerie under the bed
* Ex girlfriends in the bed
* Vagueness. Replies and grunting such as uhuh, uuuh, yeah, wot, I suppose, nah or maybe, to anything she says will result in definite no nookie situations.

Girls like your full attention.
Here's an example of how it works.

Wrong:
SHE: Shall we do something on Saturday night?
HE: (not looking up) Uhh, woh, maybe
SHE: Can't be bloomin bothered can you? I obviously mean nothing to you so I'm off to see the Dream Boys with our Elsie.
Exit girl.

Right:
SHE: Shall we do something on Saturday night?
HE: Definitely. I've already got the paper with what's on. Let's have a look through and see what you fancy?
SHE: OK, or maybe we should stay in. I've had another idea. (smirk, smoulder)

WE NEED TO TALK

Try not to go into a coma when she comes out with the inevitable "we need to talk." That fateful line that strikes dread into the male species everywhere. You've got to learn to deal with this one if you're going to be a successful sex maniac as believe me, all females come out with it some stage after the first date. It's part of their genetic programming, they can't help it.

Don't react. Say OK, fine. Practise saying this without clenching you teeth in front of a mirror 'til you've got it right. It's never as bad as it sounds and usually when she's got out whatever she has to say she'll be OK again and ready for a bit of action.

As "we need to talk" means - "I want to have a go at you for something you've done that's pissed me off," the best thing is to just listen, say you're sorry, you'll try harder in the future. That usually does the trick. Whatever you do, don't contradict her. Occasionally there are times when you can but not after the "we need talk" line. At that moment, it's definitely her show.

Seductive places:
Go for ambiance. Somewhere with a magnificent view.
You may feel that the sight of you with your keks down is a
pretty magnificent view but when it comes to girls they can be
funny and might not agree. So you have to work round to that
gently. Be generous, try a restaurant by the river, a candlelit
bistro, that sort of thing.

Right: balcony restaurant with a view of the city lights

Wrong: curried chips in the back of a van listening to the
football results

Music:
Music can play an enormous part in seduction but you have to
get it right. You can make or break the atmosphere with it.

Right: slow, smoochy stuff with love lyrics like
Je t'aime by Jane Birkin and George Gainsborough.
Barry White
Ask what her favourites are and get the cassettes

Wrong:
Psychokiller
Like a Bat out of Hell
Stand up and Fight
Lie down girl let me push it up, push it up
I've got a brand new bunch of coconuts
Hey fattie bum bum

Music can make or break
a seduction

What women want

Anticipation maybe isn't a favourite word for most men who just want to get on and get a job done, but sorry lads, it's a big word in the female dictionary, so when you do get past the kissing stage, make it a reluctant surrender.

You know it's not, you can't wait, but women love all that, being torn, tormented, withheld passion then a final give in before the big passionate scene.

Read a few romantic books for women. It's all about anticipation, holding back before the final succumbing.

Whereas a man's idea of romantic literature is wow yeah, ballistic missiles shoved in and out, massive members, her crying, ooh ahh, you're so big, you're the Master, I want it now, oohh, oh. Then both come five times.

It's a bit of a contrast to the stuff she likes, so best get genned up. Here's two examples, hers and his:

Her idea of a romantic story:

"Without mercy, he gazed deep into her soul scorching, burning his way in where no man had reached before. How could she resist? Yet she must, she must.

"Come to me," he whispered.

Though she longed to be crushed by his magnificent frame and bury herself in his strength and masculinity, she knew she must hold back.

"No, Brent, no" she murmured.

Folding her into his powerful arms, he only acknowledged her desire and soon she was abandoned in the sweet all pervading and masterful embrace that was Brent, her love, her heart."

Yeah. Bollocks I know, but girls like it.

His idea of romance:

"Her face lit up when she saw the throbbing bulge in his police uniform. Quickly slipping out of her nurses outfit, she unhooked her 38 double D cup bra.

"God you're enormous" she shuddered with delight as he shoved the pulsating **** in her juicy ****."

Slight difference huh? Read and learn.

Rules of seduction

1. Make her feel like she stands out in a crowd
2. Make her feel that she's irresistible. This can mean making an effort. Go for broke. Take her flowers but not a bunch of half dead ones that were going cheap at the local garage.

Right: A bunch of violets or freesias

Wrong: A potted pigroot

3. Leave her wanting more. First few times you see her, leave just as things are buzzing. I know it's difficult but it will pay off. She will really look forward to next time.
4. Take it slow, think unripe banana, not much fun. I know waiting isn't either but it does bear fruit.
5. There's a time to drop the cool and get enthusiastic and passionate. Girls like to know they can turn you on.
Go for it.

DREAMS

A word of warning in case you get lucky and get invited for breakfast. If you've got so far that you've got to stay the night, don't blow it in the morning by being sarcastic when she asks you about your dreams.

Wrong:
SHE: What did you dream last night?
HE: Dunno, slept right through it.

Right:
SHE: What did you dream about last night?
HE: You and me in an ocean paradise, it was wonderful. And you, what did you dream of?

And if you really want to impress her, gen up on a bit of dream interpretation.
Babies = a new beginning
Death = the end of an era and a new start
Sea = sex
Swimming = sex
Snakes = sex
Animals = one's animal nature (sex)
Naked in public = insecure (in need of more sex)

Never, ever admit you dreamt of other women.

SEX

As with the whole process, lovemaking brings out the fact that the different sexes want different things:

He wants:
* A bit of foreplay (not much, being left to watch the match in peace'll do it))
* A beer
* An orgasm
* Another beer
* A sleep

She wants:
* Hours of foreplay starting with a shopping trip and lunch by the river
* Assorted orgasms, at least one multiple, and one according to whatever's in this months Cosmo
* A cigarette
* An intimate chat and cuddle whilst looking through the latest IKEA catalogue (together)
* A mutual daydream about a garden flat with matching kitten. (Boys are expected to participate in both of these last two and can't use the time for a sneaky sleep)
* Respect.
* More foreplay
* More orgasms

He wants. She wants.

BREASTS

When she takes her clothes off, no matter how great the urge to cry "yoh great set of bazongas" or "what a pair of mazonians." Refrain. Size shouldn't matter.

It is no longer the done thing to talk about breasts in any way but with respect. So when faced by those front pieces of the body between the neck and abdomen, refrain from comment but look at them in a suitably admiring and cheerful fashion and hope that she does the same for you when faced with your protruding bits.

OK: to call this part of them breasts, mammaries, bosom or chest.

NOT OK: is any of the following: apple dumplings, begonias, chaboonis, droopers, fried eggs, gnat bites, coconuts, gazongas, jigglies, lolapaloozas, love tips, mangoes, milk churners, nompers, oojah pips, pancakes, swingers or watermelons. Oh, and baloobas is off as well.

WILLIES

If however she decides to get you back for years of ridicule
and humiliation you must take it like a man and roar with
amusement as she calls your pride and joy:

the one eyed milkman   twanger
the bat and balls   whang bone
the crown jewels   wigga wagga and the bongos
an armadillo   danglers
beef bayonet   razoos
dojigger   whennymegs
jackaroo   dong
kidneyscraper   laughing carrot
liver sausage   porridge pump
plonker   bacon roll
rhubarb   the bald headed hermit

What can you do but grin and bear it.

At least **you** never had to lie back and think of England.

Don't's:

Don't use bad language unless she starts it

Don't look around while she's telling you what pleases her

Don't fight over who sleeps which side. You can sort that out later

Don't use four letter words like don't or stop

Don't use positions that give you lockjaw

Don't use positions that make you fart. It can ruin what might be a historic moment

Don't read over her shoulder when she's making her best moves

Don't keep looking at your watch

Don't fall asleep

Don't ask did you feel the earth move? Unless you live in California

Don't give her points out of ten

Don't ask how it was for her. She might say awful

Don't laugh, point or call her Mary. Unless her name is Mary in which case it's OK

Don't snore

Don't compare her to other girls on your bed chart

Don't put her knickers on your head

Don't ask if you can keep her knickers for your collection

Don't discuss running sores (now is not the time)

And during, dont say:

Get a bloody move on

Fancy a bit of pizza

Not all girls like having their ears cleaned out during sex.

Do:
* Take your socks off first, there's nothing more ridiculous than a naked man in only his socks
* Tell your partner what pleases you. It might be anytime, any place anywhere but tell her anyway
* Do be positive not negative when you tell each other. Criticism of another's sexual technique can inhibit, so try and be encouraging. For example:

Right:
"I really like it when you do that. Could you do it a bit harder/gentler/faster/whilst swinging from that chandelier dressed as the local vicar."

Wrong:
"Yoah. Go easy you great clumsy lump."
"Stop twiddling at that like you're tuning a car radio, don't you know anything."

And remember:
Orgasm is your body's way of asking for a tea break

You are supposed to be turning on, not tuning in.

CONDOMS

Question: What do you give the girl who has everything?
Answer: Penicillin

Question: What do you call a man who uses the withdrawal method of contraception?
Answer: Daddy.

Which nicely brings us round to condoms.
Try not to think that it's like:
* eating chocolate with the wrapper on
* picking your nose with a glove on

Don't be a nerd, use them.
These days they come in all shapes and sizes. Small, medium and liar being the most popular but you can get them in all sorts of flavours. You've got to use them so might as well make them fun. Check out all the varieties. You can even get luminous ones which are particulary good for if you're a bit on the small side and in the past girls have had difficulty finding it, or if you can't see in the dark

Wear your condom with pride

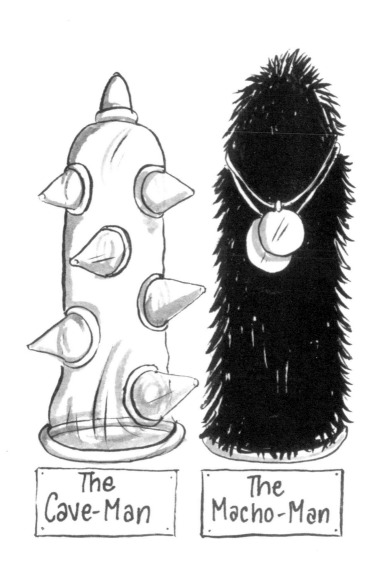

The
Cave-Man

The
Macho-Man

These days condoms come.

Super Thriller

Spotted DICK

No Hoper.

..in all shapes and sizes

ADVANCED SEX

This section is for when you're bored of the same old positions and strokes and want to try something different.
Variety is the spice, so:

* Vary the place. Have sex in dangerous places. This does not mean while parachute jumping or in a war zone. It means somewhere you might get caught at any moment like on the back of the 186 bus in the rush hour, in a box at the theatre during opera. (Particularly good if you're with a shouter as she can join in with the high notes.)
* Vary the position: go beyond 69. Seek out other spots besides the G, go for the whole A -Z in Greek, Norwegian and Sanskrit. (Don't bother with those positions that cause lock jaw or uncontrollable farting as such things can ruin the mood.)
* Vary the control. Try tying one of you up. Keep it in the house though as it's not much fun being tied to a lamppost, bus shelter or back of a moving car.
* Vary the number. Invite your friends and family to watch, comment, advise or join in.
* Vary the experience and try experimenting with any the following:

Rubber (not the washing up gloves)
Fruit (but nothing too spiky like starfruit or pineapples)
Honey/Ice-cream/anything edible and sticky.

Advanced sex speak
(for sophisticated lovers):

* Karma Sutra is a book on sexual technique. It is not a dish on an Indian menu.

* Gulam Jabi is a dish on an Indian menu. It is not a type of male sexual thrusting movement.

* Cunnilingus is a man giving a woman oral sex. It is not an airline.

* Fellatio is a woman giving a man oral sex. It is not a character in Hamlet.

* A french letter is a condom. It is not what the French use for playing scrabble.

* Safe sex isn't:
  masturbation
  when her husband's way
  sex behind locked doors.

* Oral sex is not talking about it. That is called being a prick teaser.

Fantasies to try at home
Doctors and nurses
Master and slaves
Spots and pimples (a good one if you like being squeezed)
Cowboys and Indians
Catherine the Great and big Neddie

And for those who like really strange sex try:

Unusual sexual fantasies (for the really kinky)
Guess what I'm using now your Holiness
John and Norma
Be gentle, I'm a Martian
Trainspotter meets Matron
Vicars and assorted fruit
Bill and Hilary. (And Jennifer, Shirley, Tallulah, the Blue Belle
Girls and the Local Fire Brigade)

Unerotic role playing:
Yoo hoo, I'm a tea pot
I'm E.T. and I'm in the wardrobe

Call me Betty

SAYING GOOD BYE

Sadly sometimes, things just don't work out.
Sadly sometimes, one of you just doesn't cotton on to this.
Here's few tell tale signs that let you know it's over;

* She draws round your body after you've made love then
  calls the mortuary

* You need a painkiller before you can face sex

* She finds you in bed with another woman (don't stand for
  that)

* When different bedrooms after a row becomes different
  postal codes after a row

* You feel you'd rather make love on your own

* You meet a blonde with a 44 double D chest who's wearing
  a wet T-shirt and a look that says hello sailor

* After six months you feel something is missing. You're
  right, it's July and she moved out at New Year

* You drink champagne from her shoes and choke on a corn
  plaster

* You get a letter from her saying she's living in Barcelona
  with someone else.
  And she spells your name wrong on the envelope.

Sometimes you have to be cruel to be kind

It's never easy if you're the one who has to say goodbye. Here's a few ways of making it easier, some are kinder than others:

Unkind: (but does the trick)
* Ask her to walk two steps behind when you're out
* Point to her varicose veins and say "blue just isn't my colour"
* By post from Algeria
* Get caught in an orgy with any number of page three girls
* Ask her to wash your underwear
* Put fag ash in her shoes
* Put your used chewing gum in her ear
* Ask if when she dies you can have her stuffed and put in the corner with all your other ex's as part of a Dada coat rack

If one of those doesn't work, try saying:
* My wife and kids are missing me
* I love you too much to destroy your life
* I'm embarking on a new healthy lifestyle, no fat, no alcohol, no sex (least not with you)
* I'm gay and my boyfriend has just found out about us
* Marry her (that usually kills any romance off for sure)
* I thought it was forever and that was how it felt
* I always fake my erections
* What's your name again?

But try and stay friends, all girls have friends, cousins, nieces. Stay on good terms, she may introduce you to one of them.

THE LAST WORD

Be positive.

Create your own destiny.

It worked for Henry 8th.

McNaughty
Books

McNAUGHTY BOOKS	£

The McNaughty Book of Limericks   4.99
    by Farquhar McNaughty

The McIrish Book of Logic   4.99
    by Seamus O'Really

The McVeggie Book of Rude Food   4.99
    by Squirty O'Gourd

The McTory Book of Bonks   4.99
    by Norman ffamily-Values

Victorian Cock-Ups and Other Stories   4.99
    by The Very Rev'd Steve Lovering

How to be a Politically Correct Sex Maniac   4.99
    by Johnny Condom

The Little Sexpot's Instruction Book   3.99

McNaughty Books are available from all good Book and Gift shops, or direct from the publishers John Napir Ltd. at P.O. Box 3353, London N1.